IMAGES
of England

ECCLESALL

The focal point of the district for centuries, Ecclesall church stands in a commanding position on a site which, in 1788, was known as Carter-Knoll. The building here, pictured *c.* 1850, replaced the Manor House chapel, a chapel of ease built with money donated by Ralph de Ecclesall in the thirteenth century. According to Hunter's *Hallamshire*, the new building was neat and unecclesiastical in style. In 1843 it was altered and the tower raised to its present height. In 1867 gas lighting was installed. Although seats were set aside for the poor, many of the congregation would rent pews, the money paying part of the vicar's stipend. Of the 700 seats in the 1788 church, 500 were let at an average rent of 2s per seat per annum. The pinfold, where stray animals were kept, was in front of the church and was later moved to the Rising Sun on Abbey Lane. In 1997 the church was closed for reordering, it opened once again in February 1998.

IMAGES
of England

ECCLESALL

Compiled by
Ecclesall Local History Society

TEMPUS

First published 1998
Reprinted 1999
Copyright © Ecclesall Local History Society, 1998

Tempus Publishing Limited
The Mill, Brimscombe Port,
Stroud, Gloucestershire, GL5 2QG

ISBN 0 7524 1107 1

Typesetting and origination by
Tempus Publishing Limited
Printed in Great Britain by
Midway Clark Printing, Wiltshire

Contents

Researched and compiled by Shirley Frost, Fred Peacock, Betty McPherson, Charles Hall, Mary Bramhill and Margaret Naylor. Edited by David Fenney. Project coordinated by Ethne Fox and meetings chaired by Ann Holland.

Introduction

The area known as Ecclesall has shrunk tremendously in size over the last 200 years but has increased dramatically in terms of housing and population.

A map of 1795 shows Ecclesall as stretching from a little way below the Ringinglow (a toll bar) on the north-west, right down to Cambridge Street, then known as Coal Pit Lane. Most of the south-eastern boundary followed the line of the River Sheaf as far as the fascinating old industrial complex at Abbeydale; recently taken over by the Abbeydale and Shepherd Wheel Action Trust. The River Porter formed the northern edge as far as Brocco Bank, whence the boundary stretched northwards to include parts of Broomhill and Crookesmoor.

There never was an actual village of Ecclesall. At the time of the 1795 map only the area near to Cambridge Street and the part just beyond the bottom of the Moor, known as Little Sheffield, were at all built up. Otherwise Ecclesall consisted of small hamlets and isolated farms and cottages with various small industrial works and mills along the Sheaf and Porter. According to William Fairbanks, the surveyor and cartographer, there were 296 houses in Ecclesall in 1798; considering the size of the area this was a relatively small number.

One does not nowadays connect quarrying with this part of Sheffield but as far back as the sixteenth century stone was being quarried at Brincliffe Edge. A painting by McIntyre, 'View of Sheffield from Salter's Lane, Brincliffe', shows the old cottages known as the Salt Box and a number of large grindstones awaiting transport. The fine building now standing on that spot was erected in 1911 and was originally the Bluecoat School, which provided orphan boys of Sheffield with a home and an education. After the Second World War it became the College of Art and is now the Art Department of Hallam University. Not far away is the Somerfield supermarket on Ecclesall Road, which stands in the area once occupied by another huge quarry. These and other smaller quarries provided stone for some of the earlier buildings pictured in this book and also grindstones for the small works.

It was not until much later that Ecclesall developed as a residential suburb. In the middle of the nineteenth century one could walk towards town from Ecclesall church (recently reordered) and see very few buildings. The Prince of Wales inn would have been in evidence (interestingly, after several changes, it recently reverted to its original name). Then there would be Banner Cross Hall, an imposing building of about 1817-18, built to replace an earlier Hall. Almost opposite would be Hall Farm and Hatfield House at the bottom of Ringinglow Road. Back up this road was Ecclesall National School, as the church school founded in 1834 was called at first. After that there would have been nothing down Ecclesall Road until Cedar Farm on the left and, below that, the post office.

There were a few cottages at the bottom of Psalter Lane and sixty or so years ago there existed a little shop where one could buy sherbet or liquorice bootlaces with one's Saturday penny. A bit further down was a blacksmith's forge. A steep cobbled 'gennell' linking Psalter Lane with Ecclesall Road was later associated with Charlie Peace. On the left were nothing but open fields, stretching down almost to Hunter's Bar. Here was Hunter House Farm but the only houses at that time were the terraced houses of the workers at Lescar Wheels, on the two dams in the Sharrow Vale Road area (the name survives in the Lescar Hotel).

To the east, up Ringinglow Road, there was the Hammer and Pincers inn, with its adjoining blacksmith's forge – a welcome rest for both men and horses after the steep climb from the town. A little further on was the Sun Inn (one must remember that this was the road to Manchester). On the left was the large house, Castle Dyke, and two more at Thrift House; here lived Thomas Lee who farmed in a small way, as well as having a bakery which was patronised by the pack horse trains travelling this way. A road off to the right soon brought one to Whiteley Wood Hall, a fine seventeenth-century building which had several distinguished owners over the years, including Thomas Boulsover of Sheffield Plate fame and Samuel Plimsoll, originator of the Samual Plimsoll line for the loading of ships. The Hall was demolished in 1957 but the outbuildings were converted into an outdoor activities centre for Sheffield Girl Guides.

A little further down on the right, beside Meadow Lane Farm was the small chapel (still standing) which Boulsover built for the workers at his mill on the nearby River Porter. Going back towards town one would pass a scattering of dwellings at Bents Green and Hill Top, including the original tin chapel which served the Methodists in this area, and the farm at High Storrs which had a splendid example of the old cruck-construction type of barn.

Old maps and yellowing documents tell of the early history of districts like Ecclesall, but for bringing the more recent past to life, photography is an excellent medium. Sheffield is fortunate in having had several keen photographers, including Jasper Redfern, Frank Mottershaw and Joseph Illingworth, in the early years of this century. At first outdoor photography meant carrying heavy equipment, often including a tripod, and inserting a coated glass plate into the camera for each exposure. However, in later years many ordinary citizens were using their box Brownies and folding Kodaks to record life around them and the compilers of this book are much indebted to their descendants for many of the photographs in this splendid collection.

Mary M. Bramhill

One
Ecclesall and its Hamlets

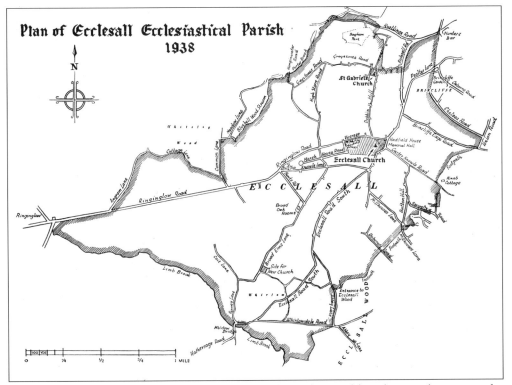

Plan of Ecclesall Ecclesiastical Parish 1938

This, generally speaking, is the area covered in this volume, although in earlier times, the Manor of Ecclesall was much larger and once stretched as far as Cambridge Street.

Hunter's Bar toll gate and house, with the dam for the Lescar Wheel on the right. Excited crowds gathered to witness the end of the toll gate at midnight on 31 October 1884. Once toll bar keeper John Speer had collected the last fee the crowd threw the gate into a nearby field.

The abolition of the toll bar at Hunter's Bar was widely reported. The toll house itself had been painted and photographed many times and Revd Cobby, writing in 1873, tells how its bow windows were filled with cakes, sweetmeats, ginger beer and lollipops. The building on the left beyond the toll house was Hunter House Farm, now part of the Hunter House Hotel.

A Cole Brothers' horse-drawn van makes its way down a tree-lined Rustlings Road around the turn of the century. In those days general drapers would deliver even the smallest article to their customers. Note the road sweepers, busy collecting fallen leaves and horse manure in an effort to keep the tram tracks free of obstruction.

The cleaning works at Onslow Road, Greystones, c. 1885. The works were taken over by W.E. Franklin after their premises at the bottom of Ecclesall Road were destroyed in the Sheffield Blitz in 1940. Franklins still occupy the premises today.

Bad times. A group of unemployed young men while away the idle hours in Endcliffe Woods in the early 1920s. Many youngsters were laid off after completing their apprenticeships in the period following the First World War.

The Holme Wheel was the middle one of the three in Endcliffe Woods. Originally the buildings housed grinding wheels but by 1903 it had become a boating pond and was also a popular spot for skating before the advent of indoor ice rinks.

Outcrop Drift
Greystones Sheffield
Coal Strike 1912.

Pictured during the coal strike of 1912, all is silence on the normally busy outcrop drift mine at Greystones. This mine entrance, or adit, is marked on the 1855 ordnance survey map and was on the hillside between High Storrs Road and Greystones Road. There are other shafts marked in the area. It was one of many small mines in the area including one at the bottom of the present Knowle Lane. This was owned by William Newbould and his family who lived at Ecclesall Old Hall at the top of what is now Millhouses Lane. He died in 1725.

Pictured are the youngsters and their parents, who lived in cottages at the bottom of Greystones Road in the early years of this century. In the 1930s the newsagent's shop was known as Dabbs. The cottages themselves survived until after the end of the Second World War.

These families lived in a row of cottages known as the Old Dove Houses between what are now Louth and Peveril Roads, off Greystones Road, in the 1890s. The cottages were pulled down in the early part of this century.

An aerial view of the Greystones area in 1980. At the beginning of this century this was mainly fields. Some of the land belonged to Greystones Hall, just off picture, centre left. The crescent of housing at the bottom of the photograph was built on the site of Brooke Bray's nursery.

Cow Lane runs behind the houses on Bingham Park Road, from Greystones Road to the top of Bingham Park. It is shown on the ordnance survey map of 1885 together with Cliffe House Farm, on the right. Behind the tree are two tiny one-up, one-down cottages which were lived in until the early 1960s.

Greystones Road in 1915, seen from the present junction with Bingham Park Road. The wall on the right surrounded the Greystones Hall estate, which was later developed for housing by the Malthouse family. The building beyond is Cliffe House Farm, home of the Wilson family from the end of the 1800s to the late 1960s, when it was demolished to make way for a small housing estate. The house on the left is Hornby Cottage. The Wilsons were dairy farmers, they delivered milk by horse and cart round the new estate.

Greystones Road, *c.* 1915. The house on the right is still there and so are the cottages behind it. Cliffe House Farm stood behind the trees on the left.

Greystones Road near the junction with High Storrs Road, *c.* 1915. The house on the right still exists but the little one on the left was demolished in the 1930s by its owner, a stonemason, and rebuilt in stone. The farm buildings and stackyard were part of Cliffe House Farm.

Salt Box Cottages on Psalter lane. Sited along the old salt route from Cheshire the cottages resembled an old tin salt container with a hinged lid, hence the name. They were the homes of quarrymen who worked the Brincliffe Quarry and were demolished in 1967.

Greystones Picture Palace in the 1920s. It was built by Henry Boot and Sons. The top entrance was to the cinema and the bottom entrance took would-be revellers down to the ballroom beneath. The premises were originally owned by Mr Rodgers whose daughter Ethel played the piano for the silent films. After her father's death she ran the cinema with her husband, Harry. The building was badly damaged by fire in later years and is now transformed as Napoleon's.

19

The Banner Cross Hotel, in 1908. Thirty years earlier, and a few yards down the road, at No. 951, Charlie Peace murdered Arthur Dyson, the husband of his lover. Thus he became one of the most notorious criminals in Sheffield's history, as well as earning a place in the national hall of infamy. He was born near Lady's Bridge in 1832 and had served four jail terms for theft and burglary before setting up in business as a picture framer and seller of musical instruments in Darnall. His neighbours were Arthur Dyson and his wife, the 'boozy, buxom' Katherine. Peace embarked on a wild affair with her until Dyson put his foot down and the married couple moved to Banner Cross. However, Charlie was persistent and on a November day in 1876 a neighbour heard Katherine scream and saw Arthur rush out of the cottage into a passage where Peace shot him before escaping across a field (now a car park). He fled to London with his wife Hannah and later shot a policeman during a burglary. He was arrested for attempted murder under the name of John Ward but his true identity became known and he was brought back to Sheffield and charged with Dyson's murder. While travelling to one hearing, he threw himself out of the train at Darnall (while travelling at 50mph) but was recaptured. He was tried at Leeds town hall in 1879. The jury took just ten minutes to convict him and he was sentenced to death. He then confessed to having killed a policeman during a burglary in Manchester – thereby saving the life of a young Irishman who had already been convicted of that crime.

THE NOTORIOUS BLACKHEATH BURGLAR.

PEACE,

THE MURDERER OF Mr. ARTHUR DYSON, Civil Engineer, Banner Cross, Sheffield, November, 1876.

A portrait of Charlie Peace. Despite losing some fingers in a rolling mill accident, Charlie was quite an accomplished violinist and was dubbed 'the modern Paganini.' On the morning of his execution he complained of his last breakfast: 'This is bloody rotten bacon.' He wrote his own epitaph: 'In memory of Charles Peace, who was executed in Armley Prison, Tuesday, February 25, 1879. For that I done but never intended.'

21

Knab Farm was the home of Mr Denniff who, as well as farming, was a well known butcher. In the 1960s this land was sold for housing development and the Knab Farm Estate, built by Gleesons, rose on these acres. Brincliffe Edge Road can be seen beyond the farmhouse.

The fields below Banner Cross Hall before the building of the Knab Farm Estate. Below the woods on Brincliffe Edge Road are the allotments where episodes of the TV series *I Didn't Know You Cared* were filmed.

Cherry Tree Farm and cottages, c. 1900. This is the site of the Cherry Tree pub at the junction of Carterknowle Avenue. The three cherry trees were reduced to stumps in the pub's rockery.

This is an old print of Ecclesall chapel, a chapel of ease in the parish of Sheffield. It was replaced by a new building in the eighteenth century and the present church was developed from that.

A welcome sight for thirsty travellers, along the wheel-rutted Ecclesall Road of those days, was the Prince of Wales Hotel which was built around 1808, reputedly with stones from the old Ecclesall chapel. It was said to have 'ample accommodation' for people wishing to break their journey.

The Prince of Wales in the days of Mr Hollingsworth, who poses proudly in the doorway beneath the board bearing his name. In 1928 the inn was rebuilt in mock Tudor style. In the 1980s it was revamped into an Amercan-style diner and renamed the Woodstock. In the early 1990s it suffered for a time under the title of the Real Macaw. It finally reverted to its original name in 1998, much to the satisfaction and relief of the locals.

The rear of the Prince of Wales Hotel towards the end of the last century. There were tea rooms and a bowling green that later became a car park.

A truly rural scene in Ecclesall, in the 1800s. The parish church, without chancel and transept which were added in 1906-8, looks down on a peaceful main road. A wagon laden with logs is halted while the harness of one of the horses is adjusted. Perhaps it is the driver, on the right, who is taking advantage of the delay to flirt with the girl tying a bundle of sticks.

Members of the congregation of Ecclesall parish church gather for morning service on a winter's day, c. 1903. At this time the lychgate was the main entrance to the church.

In 1829 Fairbanks, the renowned surveyors, drew up plans for a smithy and house on waste land fronting onto Millhouses Lane and the Hathersage turnpike, now Ecclesall Road South. It was built for Guite Mottram, to replace his smithy across the way above Ecclesall Hall Farm, near what is today Woodholm Road. The Mottrams were a very old local family who had farmed at Trap Lane, Hill Top and for many generations at Ecclesall Hall Farm.

Charles Reaney was the last blacksmith to run the shoeing forge, which was later taken over by the farm and used to store hay. Subsequently the house and smithy were pulled down and in 1914 the builder Walter Ramsay erected Montgomery House on the site for himself and his family (see page 28).

Walter Ramsay in front of his new home with his wife and children. Behind them are the housekeeper, chauffeur and other servants. He sold the house to Dr Wilson. It later became a children's nursery and in 1977 was demolished, to be replaced by a large block of flats – Montgomery Court.

The bottom of Knowle Lane, in 1924. For years a favourite walk with local people was to Bents Green from Ecclesall Hall Road, now Woodholm Road. They began by climbing the stile on the right and then followed a path through the fields to Hill Top. Next to the stile was the boundary wall of Weetwood House, then the home of Sir William Ellis and his family. To the left was Ecclesall Manor House, barely visible through the trees. The house now accommodates offices.

The Archway, Dobbin Hill in 1915. This was the home of Mr Slater, Sunday school superintendent at Ecclesall parish church, and his family. The rear of the building looked out over a field of Haslam's Farm, now Falkland Road, where the annual Whit Sings and sports day were held.

In 1840 there lived at Button Hill; two shopkeepers, one stonemason, one teapot handle maker and five farmers. The area of the road near Carterknowle was known as Lane Ends. The cottages were pulled down in the post-war years.

Milking time at High Storrs. This area just below High Storrs Road was known on the old map as High Lane Head. Over the years the cows disappeared and houses were built along Huntley Road and Ringinglow Road.

Silver Hill Nursery, off Knowle Lane was a popular centre for gardeners. The centre was run by Len and Bill Etchells, who took the business over from Sheffield Horticultural Nurseries in 1947. In later years the land was taken over to use for housing development.

High Storrs Farm stood opposite High Storrs school until its demolition in 1966. The last owner was Miss Ann Robinson.

This ancient cruck barn was also lost when High Storrs Farm was knocked down to make way for housing.

Bents Green, originally Hill Top, is still a closely-knit community and many of the families have lived there for generations. This shows the huddle of buildings between Trap Lane and Bents Green Road, *c.* 1910. These were demolished in the thirties to make way for the present parade of shops. Originally, standing where the post office is now, was Mrs Fanny Wilkins' sweet shop, next door lived Mrs Selina Chidgey who baked and served afternoon tea in her front room on Saturdays, next was a blacksmith's shop, then the entrance to the stockyard of Fearn's Farm. On Trap Lane corner was Mrs Mary Royles' general store.

Bents Yard in 1920. The cluster of four cottages with a barn in the middle was situated almost at the top of Bents Road, where it levels out. Lawrence Hancock, who later had the garage, ran his corn chandlery from the rear of one of the cottages. The cottage at the back belonged to Harry Barker, a file maker. He had a magnificent pear tree which was a prime target for scrumpers.

A view of Bents Green looking in the opposite direction in 1915. The white house on the left was built in 1788 by John Hill. In 1913 it was bought by Lawrence Hancock and used as a corn chandler's and grocery shop until the start of the Second World War. For many years Mr Medley and his wife, Mr Hancock's daughter, ran a garage in the grounds of the old house until it was sold by auction in 1990. Today there are flats on the car servicing area and offices in the house.

These cottages at Chapel Yard, Trap Lane, Bents Green date back 300 years. The buildings are pictured in the 1960s. Shortly afterwards the cottages, along with those at the rear in Latham Square, were pulled down and replaced by old people's flats. The occupiers of these cottages, starting with No. 1 on the left, were: Mrs Poll Thompson, Henry Outram, David Clark and family, Wilf and Emma Clark, Sarah Needham, Henry Hancock, Mrs Ethel Hancock and Joshua and Lois Needham.

The Hammer and Pincers with its old smithy, *c.* 1904. Situated on the old turnpike road, it was the home to generations of the Osborne family in the nineteenth century and their skills as blacksmiths were in great demand. Part of the building became a hostelry in the 1820s with Joseph Osborne as landlord, but with the advent of the motor car the forge gradually fell into disuse and in 1958 it was converted into the Smithy Bar. The cottage in the background, on the left, was part of Bents Yard, a cluster of cottages on Bents Road.

Snow is piled high around the Hammer and Pincers in 1947, one of the worst winters this century. By then it was selling Mappins beers. Now it is a Bass Charrington pub.

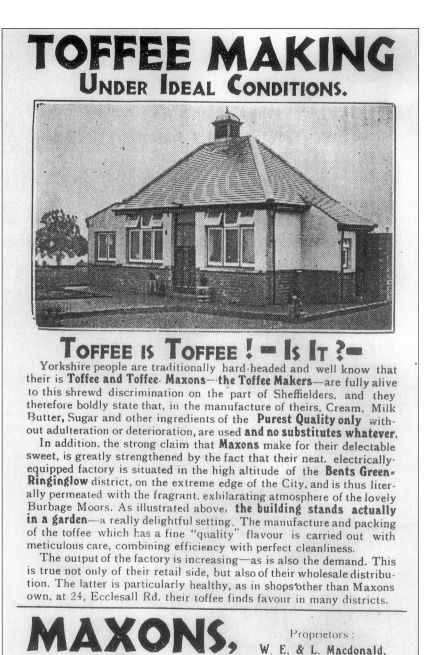

TOFFEE MAKING
UNDER IDEAL CONDITIONS.

TOFFEE IS TOFFEE ! — IS IT ? —

Yorkshire people are traditionally hard-headed and well know that their is **Toffee and Toffee.** **Maxons—the Toffee Makers—**are fully alive to this shrewd discrimination on the part of Sheffielders, and they therefore boldly state that, in the manufacture of theirs, Cream, Milk Butter, Sugar and other ingredients of the **Purest Quality only** without adulteration or deterioration, are used **and no substitutes whatever.**

In addition, the strong claim that **Maxons** make for their delectable sweet, is greatly strengthened by the fact that their neat, electrically-equipped factory is situated in the high altitude of the **Bents Green-Ringinglow** district, on the extreme edge of the City, and is thus literally permeated with the fragrant, exhilarating atmosphere of the lovely Burbage Moors. As illustrated above, **the building stands actually in a garden**—a really delightful setting. The manufacture and packing of the toffee which has a fine "quality" flavour is carried out with meticulous care, combining efficiency with perfect cleanliness.

The output of the factory is increasing—as is also the demand. This is true not only of their retail side, but also of their wholesale distribution. The latter is particularly healthy, as in shops other than Maxons own, at 24, Ecclesall Rd. their toffee finds favour in many districts.

MAXONS,
Redg.

Proprietors :
W. E. & L. Macdonald,

BENTS GREEN GARDEN FACTORY
And 24 ECCLESALLL ROAD, SHEFFIELD
'Phones : 23400. & 31819.

A toffee factory in Ecclesall? Suprisingly there was – the Bents Green Garden Factory of Maxon's, proprietors W.E. and L. Macdonald. They also had a shop on Ecclesall Road. The factory was situated in Latham Square, off Trap Lane. In their publicity Maxon's claimed the quality of their toffee was enhanced because 'their neat, electrically equipped' factory was sited on the extreme edge of the city and was 'literally permeated with the fragrant, exhilarating atmosphere of the lovely Burbage Moors'. It closed during the Second World War.

This splendid old horse trough originally stood on a site near the present roundabout at Hunters Bar. It is said to have been placed there by the Wilsons of the Snuff Mill, in memory of Henry Wilson. It was later moved to a field on Cottage Lane, where it aroused the interest of passers-by for many years. It is currently awaiting a new home.

The bottom of Trap Lane, which was probably a pack horse trail once and is one of the oldest roads in Sheffield. Off to the right, below the trees is an old drift mine.

This venerable yew tree at Thrift House is believed to be the oldest living thing in Sheffield and might be as much as 800 years old. In medieval times yew trees were used as signposts or boundary markers and the Monks' Guides were seven yews which marked the way for the monks as they travelled up Millhouses Lane from the Abbey to Ecclesall chapel.

Biddy the Lakeland Terrier enjoys a cool drink from the stone trough at the right hand side of the drive to Thrift House in the late 1940s. Water from a stream was collected by householders from a series of troughs which were fed by natural gravity. Many people swore that the water worked as a cure for their children's whooping cough. The stream flowed by Plumpton Cottages, then ran down the hillside through the Brookfields to a trough at Parkhead. The stream can still be seen in the gardens of Bents Drive, Hill Turrets and by Parkhead post office.

In 1895 Garden Cottage on the Old Broad Oak Green, near to Shaw House, was the home of Mr and Mrs R. Brassington. Plums were widely grown in the area and Garden Cottage was noted for its plum trees. Miss Brassington married Lawrence Hancock and they ran the shop in the White House at Bents Green.

Farmer's wife, Sarah Needham, feeds the hens during the hot summer of 1921 at Broad Oak Farm. The farm was at the corner of what is now Bents Drive and Broad Elms Lane. Her husband Frank was injured in the First World War and in 1926 they had to leave the farm to live in a cottage in Chapel Yard, Hill Top.

View at Park Head. HbS.818.

haw House was the home of John haw, a clothier and weaver, in 635. It was rebuilt in 1830 for a armer, William Bartin, who added n a cutler's shop where files were nade. In time Joseph Orbell, Earl itzwilliam's huntsman, retired here and his two daughters ran a lame-school on the premises. The ouse was again restored in recent ears with the barns being added on o the main building.

One of the oldest roads in the district, Broad Elms Lane is pictured in 1924, before Alms Hill Road was constructed and prior to the spate of building that took place in the 930s. The buildings just visible on he left comprised Alms Hill Farm, which was known locally as Hulley's Farm. Before the advent of the motor car the steep part of the lane was a favourite with tobogganers.

Parkhead is pictured in the early years of this century, with its cluster of picturesque cottages on the left and the old Wheatsheaf Inn on the right. Note the very narrow Abbey Lane, or Wood Lane as it was known locally. Although fairly isolated with little traffic, Parkhead had a sub post office, grocer's, Temperance Society café and reading room and a glass-eye maker's.

Parkhead post office and grocery, c. 1905. At this time it was run by George Greenfield. It is, however, Mr and Mrs Potts, who ran the shop for over forty years from whom many will remember buying their humbugs and gobstoppers as children. The far cottage was where Mr J Corker ran his Scientific Glass business, making glass eyes for the many people who had been disabled in the First World War.

A horseman and his dog outside the old Wheatsheaf Inn at Parkhead *c*. 1904, when the landlord was Fred Oakes. Coaches stopped here on their way to Castleton. Next to the pub was a smithy that later became a garage. The old inn was pulled down in 1928 to make way for the present hostelry.

These old cottages at Parkhead, seen in 1939, were scheduled as a clearance area under a compulsory purchase order from the city council. There were many protests, including one from the Council for the Preservation of Rural England, but to no avail. The lane between the cottages and the post office was known as Back Lane and joined the field path to Alms Hill Farm.

The Whirlow Bridge Inn was built around 1846 on the curve of an old turnpike road. Originally a beer house, it had an attractive double frontage, stabling and was a pleasant place for travellers to stop. In the 1920s it became a favourite oasis for walkers from the city as there was little traffic and the area was still very rural. However, the landlord lost his licence and the inn was then converted into use as tea rooms. It later became a private residence and was demolished in August 1938.

Whirlow Bridge, in the winter of 1948. Following the demolition of the inn in 1938 Sir Walter Benton Jones, who lived at Whirlow Brook, decided to build two houses on the site for his staff. Ecclesall Road South was eventually straightened and the dangerous bend on the old turnpike road, scene of many accidents, became a quiet backwater.

The notorious bend on the Hathersage Road, known as the Devil's Elbow, is seen during construction work, *c.* 1920.

In 1930 the 'Elbow' was straightened and widened. The track of the old road can still be seen here.

The Yardley grave has been a well known feature of Ecclesall Woods for more then 200 years. George Yardley, a charcoal burner, was burned to death in his cabin on 11 October 1786 after a night out at the nearby Rising Sun. This memorial was erected by the innkeeper, Sampson Brookshaw and others. The existence of the wood is recorded as far back as 1319, it provided work for local men for centuries as charcoal was in great demand by the iron and steel industries. The woods were opened to the public in 1928.

Two

Notable Homes
and Gardens

By the middle of the nineteenth century Sheffield's captains of industry no longer had to live 'over the shop' and were preparing to spend some of their fortunes on residences of a standard to reflect their hard-won status. They looked towards the rolling green fields of Ecclesall, where the prevailing south-westerly winds would keep the smoke and fumes of their factories at bay. Here they built their mansions and surrounded them with landscaped grounds. Most of them are now no more. One of the houses that survived was Whirlow Brook Hall, pictured here and on page 63.

Banner Cross Hall, now the headquarters of Henry Boot and Sons, was originally designed for General Murray in 1817 by the famous architect Jeffrey Wyatt. Wyatt, although he worked on Windsor Castle and Chatsworth, regarded the Hall as one of his finest achievements. It replaced a residence built in Tudor times for the Bright family, who are said to have given rest and refreshment to Mary Queen of Scots on her way to confinement in Sheffield Castle. General Murray had intended to modernise the dilapidated Hall but he was persuaded to demolish instead and start anew. Sadly he died before it was completed and the estate was inherited by his sister, Ann Bagshawe. It was sold to Charles Boot in the 1930s.

For many years prior to 1932 the Hall was leased to several notable Sheffield families including four Master Cutlers; George Wilson, Douglas Vickers, Lt Col H.K. Stephenson and David Flather (who is pictured on the back row, second from the left). The others pictured on the back row, from left to right are: Kenneth Flather, Kitty Flather, Walter Brook, Maud Flather, Edith Brook. Front row, from left to right: Phoebe Flather, Laura Flather, Edmond Mainprize.

Any devotees of Richmal Crompton's *Just William* books may be reminded of their scruffy hero by this photograph of a rather formidable array of matriarchs. The little boy and girl are dressed up and on their best behaviour – a scornful William, off camera, could be the focus of those piercing eyes! Actually, this shows Mrs David Flather, then Mistress Cutler, receiving some flowers as she opens the Christmas exhibition and sale of works of art by the disabled men of Painted Fabrics Ltd in December 1926.

Another Flather family group pose on the terrace wall built by Wyatt. From left to right: Simon Forrest, Ruth Flather, Robert Waterhouse, Jill Waterhouse, Kenneth Flather.

This tower, set into the ten foot high wall at the bottom of Ringinglow Road, which bounded the kitchen gardens of Banner Cross Hall, was built for Lord John Murray as a bolt hole to afford him some peace and quiet. It included two rooms with bow windows and he is said to have kept a small library there.

Castle Dyke is thought to be on the site of an ancient camp or early settlement. When Thomas Kershaw leased Castle Dyke Farm from the Hollis Trust in 1829 there were stables, a coach house, outbuildings and gardens. Kershaw was required to spread on the land 'such compost or manure necessary to produce satisfactory crops'. At some time towards the turn of the century Castle Dyke was either enlarged or rebuilt into a substantial gentleman's residence. In 1900 Ernest Hague bought the estate from the Hollis Trust for £5,750. In 1943 Sheffield Corporation purchased the estate together with 194 acres of land and in 1946 it became a residential home. In 1989 Castle Dyke, with 4.1 acres of land, was sold at auction for £835,000 and is now a private residence once again.

These old farm buildings at Silver Hill are believed to be the last remnants of Ecclesall Hall and were the home of Gervase Strelley, Lord of the Manor of Ecclesall in the early part of the seventeenth century. It was possibly built on the site of the former Ecclesall Hall, home of the De Ecclesall family. After the death of Gervase, the lords of the Manor of Ecclesall lived elsewhere.

After its loss of status it is possible that the manor house was reduced in size and converted into a farmhouse. There is no doubt that the farm buildings were of great age. The Revd Cobby, writing in 1873, mentions its ancient appearance and the existence of a date stone for 1602. The farm was demolished in August 1935.

50

Grange Cliffe on Button Hill was a lovely gabled house, set in more than twelve acres of land with spectacular views over the then unspoiled countryside. It was built by Thomas Creswick and later became the home of Colonel and Mrs W. Tozer, whose daughter Pauline was to marry the famous cricket commentator Brian Johnston. Colonel Tozer was Master Cutler in 1936. The house was demolished in 1935 to make way for the building of Kingsley Park Grove.

Greystones Hall was built, c. 1800, for Samuel Greaves the grocer. It replaced the old Hall built by the Brights 200 years earlier. The mortar was said to have been mixed with treacle which, when combined with sand and lime, was one of the best cures for damp. The Hall remains standing today as Greystones Hall Rest Home.

Hill Turrets stood on the corner of Bents Road and Ecclesall Road and was approached through fine ornamental gates with a lodge on the right. This imposing house was set in beautiful gardens. There were ten bedrooms on the first floor. After the Second World War it became too big for a family home and was taken over by the Coal Board until 1957. It then remained empty until being demolished in 1963 – bequeathing its name to the housing estate built on the site.

This lovely, creeper-clad house took its name from the old name for Bents Green; Hill Top. It faced the Hammer and Pincers pub. The land in which the house was set stretched down to Bents Green Lodge. For a number of years it was the home of Mr and Mrs Norman Bennett. He was the founder of Bennett's College, a well known commercial college in Melbourne Avenue. The house was eventually pulled down and replaced by flats.

Holly Court, on Millhouses Lane, was built by Frederick Arthur Kelley, a brewer, c. 1895. Set in nineteen acres of land it was renowned for its gardens and woods and when Paul Kuehnrich bought the estate in 1912 he enhanced its reputation even further. He was said to have employed nine gardeners and in the spring of 1926 put a notice in the newspaper inviting people to view the 'wondrous' sight of the daffodils. Snaithing Woods, part of the estate, contained a lake and bathing pool. The house was demolished around 1970 and the stables have now been converted into a house.

Holly Court was put up for auction in the 1930s, after the death of Mr Kuehnrich. Special mention was made of the entrance hall with its oak panelling, marble pillars and parquet floor. There was also an unusually fine bathroom comprising a massive bath and walls of marble.

The famous daffodils in the wood at Holly Court. The public were invited to come and admire them. The scene was featured on postcards of the time.

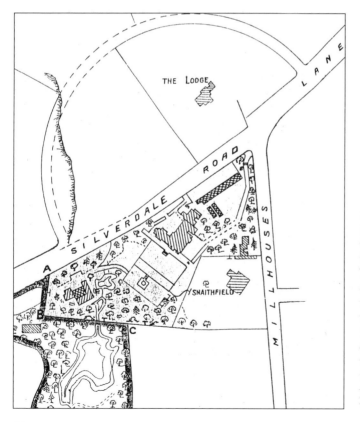

A section of the map from the sale plan of Holly Court, when it was put up for auction on 12 July 1932. The map also shows a house called The Lodge which was demolished to make way for a block of flats, those flats retained the original name. Snaithfield was another large house in the area which, again, was pulled down and replaced with houses.

Peacocks strut the lawns in this drawing of Holmwood, a mansion built in local Derbyshire gritstone for Henry Vickers, *c.* 1864. The house stands on a gently sloping hill with splendid views over Ecclesall Woods to the Derbyshire hills. It was once approached through elegant gates and down a long carriage drive which became Cortworth Road in this century.

In 1925 Joshua Needham was a fourteen year old stable boy at Holly Court. This picture was taken with Prince in a nearby field.

Mylnhurst was built in 1883, by Major William Greaves Blake. Blake, after the death of his first wife, married Rebecca Jessop the daughter of Thomas Jessop, founder of The Jessop Hospital for Women and a steel baron who served as Master Cutler and mayor in 1863. Mylnhurst was renowned for its beautiful gardens complete with lake, Japanese garden, greenhouses and vinery. Part of the land was sold for housing on Button Hill and Millhouses Lane and the lake was filled in. After Mrs Blake's death the house was sold to Mr W.J. Walsh, the draper who owned Walsh's department store on High Street. In 1933 it became Mylnhurst School. The tall chimney stacks had to be removed after they were badly damaged in a gale in 1962.

Button Hill House, No. 1 Wood Rolm Road. When Philip Blake planned to marry Dorothy Barbour his father gave him a piece of Mylnhurst land, the house was constructed there in 1908. It was sold in 1936 to the Sisters of Mercy who used it as a boarding house for Mylnhurst pupils. Later, and by now known as St Gerard's, it housed noviciates and then became university lodgings. Eventually it was demolished to make way for bungalows.

My hat! The height of fashion is displayed at the wedding of Philip Jessop Blake and Dorothy Barbour on 17 June 1908.

The roof and chimneys of Thrift House off Ringinglow Road can be seen above the trees in this peaceful scene in 1947. The first Thrift House had been built centuries previously. In 1686 Robert and Richard Offerton erected a substantial home. It was rebuilt in 1840 and enlarged in 1883, at this time the architect noted that the extremely thick walls in the middle of the house dated from a period much earlier than the rest.

An earlier photograph of Thrift House decked out in snow. In the days when the pack horse trains travelled along Ringinglow they would buy their bread supplies from the bakery at the house.

This well known landmark overlooking the junction of Knowle Lane and Ecclesall Road South has a long and chequered history. It was originally Ecclesall College but when the school closed in 1880 the building was purchased by Mr Crossley, who renamed it The Knowle. He lived there until 1892 when it was bought by a steel manufacturer, John Kingsford Wilson, who called it Kingscote. The next owner, in 1907, was Sir William Ellis, managing director of John Brown and Son. He gave the house the name Weetwood. After his death in 1945 it was sold to Sheffield Corporation and opened as Ecclesall branch library, seen here in 1980. However, in 1995, in the face of fierce local opposition, it was sold and converted into a pub and restaurant. In May 1998 it reopened as a restaurant and bar under a new name…The Old Library. It is also the meeting place for Ecclesall Local History Society.

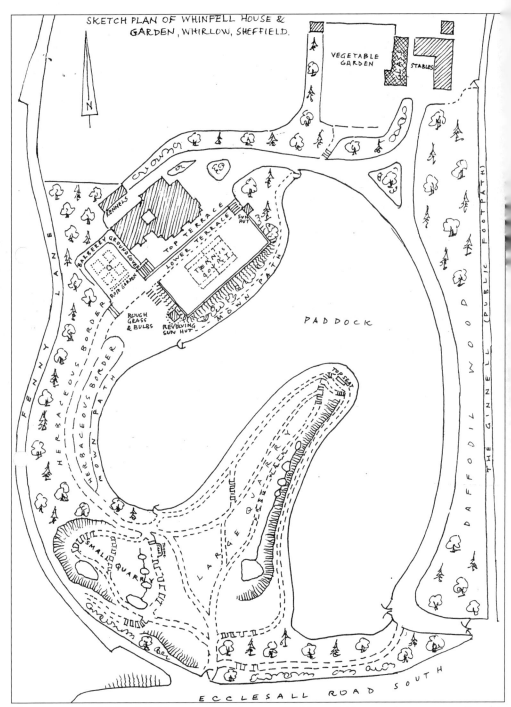

This is a map of Whinfell House and gardens at Whirlow Bridge, as they were earlier this century. Whinfell was built for the industrialist Samuel Doncaster and his family who settled in around 1902. Tragically the house was gutted by fire in 1971; it was fully demolished in 1979 and the land used for housing. Fortunately, the quarry gardens he created remain for all to enjoy.

An evocative scene, *c.* 1902. This is from the Doncaster family album and shows them enjoying a picnic with their cousins the Barbers, shortly after moving into their new home. These affairs were organised with some style, note the tablecloth, kettle, milk jugs and teapot. Although an informal occasion, hats were worn. Samuel Doncaster is on the front row, third from the left and his wife is in the centre.

Samuel Doncaster and his wife, Emma Gertrude, in the 1930s. He was a keen naturalist and gardener and by the time the family were settled in, he had transformed a large quarry on the land with the help of Backhouse of York. In 1912 he asked Clarence Elliott, destined also to become a famous nurseryman, to design and plant a smaller quarry. When the Neill family moved into Whinfell they carried out major replantings and after Sir Frederick Neill's death, the quarry gardens were donated to the city in his memory.

The quarry gardens today. They still have two of California's giant redwood trees, which well travelled Samuel brought to the country as seeds. The gardens are now in a semi-wild state which, according to his grandson, was 'exactly how Samuel would have liked them'.

Whirlow Brook is known today to many thousands of visitors who come to walk in the lovely grounds, enjoy a cup of tea or attend one of the many functions held at what is known as Whirlowbrook Hall. The Hall was built as a family home by Mr and Mrs Percy Fawcett, c. 1906. When they moved to Dore Manor House in 1920 Mr Fawcett's sister, Madge, and her husband moved in.

Like Whinfell, the beautiful gardens of Whirlow Brook were designed by the famous landscape nurseryman, Backhouse of York. The rock garden and lake form one of the glories of the park in spring and autumn. In 1946 Mr Benton Jones, now Sir Walter, sold Whirlow Brook with its 39½ acres of land. The Town Trust, Graves Charitable Trust and Sheffield Corporation bought it for £15,000. Whirlow Brook Park was opened to the public in 1951.

The original Whiteley Wood Hall was built in the sixteenth century for the wealthy Mitche
family. The building pictured here was built by Alexander Ashton in 1662, to overlook th
valley of the Porter Brook. In the ensuing years many well known Sheffield families were to liv
there, including Thomas Boulsover, the discoverer of Sheffield Plate, and Samuel Plimsof
inventor of the safety loading line for ships. After many attempts to save it, the Hall wa
demolished in 1957 but the grounds and outbuildings are still used by the Girl Guide
Association.

Between 1911 and 1926 Whiteley Wood Hall was the home of William Clark, managing director of Vickers, who lived there with his wife, son Willie and daughter May. This photograph comes from their family album.

May Clark with her fiancé Eric Moxey (left), brother Willie and some friends during the First World War. Willie was later killed on the Somme. May married Eric who pioneered the techniques of bomb disposal in the Second World War and became the first RAF officer to be awarded the George Cross. He was killed defusing a bomb that had been dropped on Biggin Hill airfield in August 1940.

May Clark (left), with her fiancé Eric Moxey and a friend. They are boating on the small lake in the grounds of the Hall. The lake was also used for skating – after the gardener's boy had first tested the strength of the ice! The Guides Association now use the lake for canoeing and rafting.

The gardener, Mr Davis, was at work in the walled kitchen garden which lay behind the stables and his cottage. The Hall was self-sufficient in vegetables, fruit and flowers and each morning cook sent her list of requirements for the day. Peaches and melons were grown in large greenhouses and there was a vinery and a tropical house heated by a stove in the wall.

Three
Schools

Ecclesall National School was founded under a deed of gift from Earl Fitzwilliam in 1834, for the education of children and adults, or children only, of the 'labouring and poorer classes' in the township of Ecclesall.

Boys square up to each other, play cricket and even appear to be fencing in this very early view of the playing fields, now allotments, of Ecclesall College. The house, which many years later became Ecclesall public library and is now the Old Library Restaurant, was built in 1858 to rehouse the boys' school known as Stone Grove in the Glossop Road area of the city. The principal, Dr John Munro and his wife, Catherine, ran the school together and renamed it Ecclesall College. After the doctor's death in 1866 his widow continued as proprietress with Samuel Downing Roome as headmaster. The college closed in 1880.

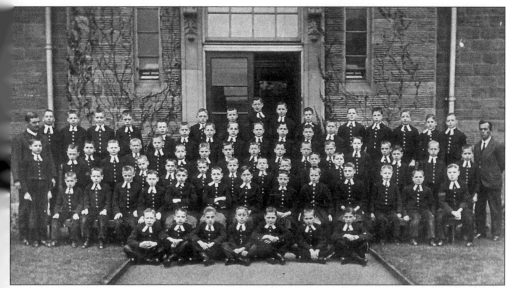

Pupils of the Bluecoats School in 1918, wearing their full uniform of long blue coats buttoned in front and cut away behind, with yellow braid, brass buttons, green corduroy trousers, yellow stockings and white bands. They also had blue muffin caps. The charity school was founded in 1706 when ten boys were taught at Shrewsbury Hospital. Later a school was built by public subscription on a site in East Parade. It transferred to Psalter Lane in 1911 and closed at the outbreak of war in 1939. In following years it was used as a training centre for the Royal Army Service Corps and finally became the College of Art in 1950 when the buildings and land were bought for £40,500.

Boys of Bluecoats School, some wearing football kit, in 1911. With them are the headmaster, Mr Bonson (right) and his assistant Mr Graham. Another noted headmaster of the school for twenty-four years was William Ball.

Standards Four and Five at Ecclesall Church of England School, in the 1924-25 school year.

Madam.
To the most noble Marquis of H—
My Lord Marquis Your Lordship
To the Right Honorable the Earl of B—
My Lord, Your Lordship.
To His Grace The Lord Archbishop.
My Lord Arch—; Your Grace.

History Notes

3 Britains
1. Brittany — France, Bretons
2 Great Britain
3 Greater Britain
3 Englands
1. Old England Schleswig
2. England
3 New England - America
First Inhabitants — Britons
1st Invasion - Romans 55 B.C. } Julius Cæsar
2nd   "   "   54 B.C. }
3rd   "   "   43 A.D.

A page from the exercise book of Alice Carr, a pupil in class VII in 1900.

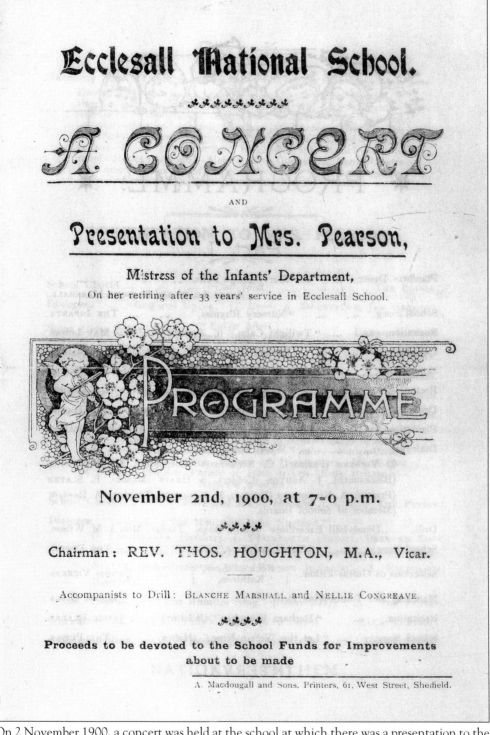

Ecclesall National School.

✿✿✿✿✿✿✿✿

A CONCERT

AND

Presentation to Mrs. Pearson,

Mistress of the Infants' Department,

On her retiring after 33 years' service in Ecclesall School.

PROGRAMME

November 2nd, 1900, at 7=0 p.m.

✿✿✿

Chairman: REV. THOS. HOUGHTON, M.A., Vicar.

Accompanists to Drill: BLANCHE MARSHALL and NELLIE CONGREAVE.

✿✿✿

Proceeds to be devoted to the School Funds for Improvements about to be made

A. Macdougall and Sons, Printers, 61, West Street, Sheffield.

On 2 November 1900, a concert was held at the school at which there was a presentation to the head of the infant's department, Mrs Pearson, who was retiring after thirty-three years of service.

The staff of the Central School, later to become High Storrs School, pose outside their building in Orchard Lane in 1903. The school moved to High Storrs thirty years later and the Orchard Lane premises were taken over by the Pupil Teachers' Centre, which later became the City Grammar School.

May Day celebrations in 1905 for the girls' department of the Central School. The May Queen that year was Matilda Borland, Queen Violet, who later taught at High Storrs until her retirement in 1949. The celebrations took place in the yard behind the education offices. The May Day tradition continued in High Storrs until 1940.

The coach of the Lord Mayor of London passes along Ecclesall Road in 1933 as it carries the Lord Mayor and Lady Mayoress to the opening of High Storrs School. Their arrival was delayed by an hour as the horses found Ringinglow Road too steep, so the whole procession had to be diverted up Bents Road.

This is a family group. Mr Fred Lee and his wife Susan, on the extreme left and right, were the caretakers at Greystones School in the early 1900s and all nine of their children helped them at the one time or another. The headmaster at the time was Mr Gould, a strict disciplinarian but well liked. The school was taken over as a hospital in the First World War but was reinstated as Greystones Intermediate School in 1924.

The class of 1921-22 at Greystones Council School.

Looking remarkably cheerful considering the ordeal ahead are these members of the fourth year at Greystones Secondary School, in 1948. They would soon be taking their School Certificate exams. Mrs Marjorie Delgarno (née Richmond), who provided this photograph, is pictured on the third row from the back, third from the left. She retired from playground duties at the school in 1998.

Pictured with her court is seven-year-old
Susan Mollie Hartle, who was crowned
the 1922 May Queen at Greystones
School. She was elected by her fellow
pupils and remembers enjoying a
wonderful day, country dancing and
winding coloured ribbons round the
maypole. Her class teacher was Miss
Hobson and the headmistress at the time
was Miss Anthonies.

Mollie, now Mrs Wyles. She was crowned
May Queen by Coun Gertrude Wilkinson
who gave her an autograph book
containing the quotation, 'True worth is
in being not seeming', a standard which,
Mollie says, she has always tried to live
up to.

Sheffield was a pioneer of the open-air school in this country and the first was opened at Whiteley Woods, in what was the old village school, in June 1909. The children gathered at the tramcar station near the education offices in Leopold Street and travelled by special tram to the Ecclesall terminus, where two wagonettes waited to take them uphill to the school. In the evening the children walked back to the terminus and arrived back in the city centre at 6.45p.m. or slightly earlier in the winter.

A physical education class at Whiteley Woods, in the 1960s. The school later became an outdoor activity centre but was eventually sold and has now been converted into a private residence.

A major factor in the setting up of the school was the growth of the school medical service. The health of children in Sheffield was as bad as, if not worse than the health of children in other major industrial cities. The first pupils were found to be suffering mainly from anaemia and malnutrition, though some had TB. Feeding them was an important part of the school day and meals, planned with the Domestic Science School, cost just under 2s 6d per child per week with plenty of soups and stews. Here an open-air class is at work.

Two of the three open-air schools in Sheffield, at Whiteley Woods and Bents Green, were still fully operational in the 1960s and catering for delicate children. Here some of the Whiteley Woods pupils enjoy themselves on climbing frames.

The kindergarten class of Mylnhurst School, in 1958. Mylnhurst was bought from department store owner, W.J. Walsh, in 1933 by the Sisters of Mercy in order to open a school catering for the Catholic community of Ecclesall. It began with seven pupils and was originally known as Mylnhurst High School – changing later to Mylnhurst Convent School. By 1935 there were 96 pupils including 10 boarders and the old billiard room had become a dining room and music room. Since those early days a chapel, swimming pool, nursery and gymnasium have been added.

The first boarders of Mylnhurst are seen wearing their outdoor uniforms in the mid-1930s.

Divine guidance for the Sisters of Mercy as they engage in some extracurricular activity, tending the gardens of Mylnhurst on a spring afternoon.

Due to overcrowding in schools in the 1950s, partly fuelled by the post-war baby boom, Ecclesall Church School had to find somewhere to house the overflow and in 1952 the new county infants school was built off High Storrs Road. Before it was opened, junior three children at the church school were taken by bus to Totley County School. In 1956 Silverdale School was built and a number of older Ecclesall children were based there for a time. In 1969 Dobcroft Junior was built and the pressures on Ecclesall Church School were finally removed.

The old school and schoolhouse on Broad Elms Lane. It was a school for almost 200 years before becoming a mission hall in the first part of this century. Later it was converted into a private school, Ecclesall High School, but the buildings were severely damaged in the gale of February 1962 and the school was forced to close. The buildings were later restored and converted into flats.

Four
Transport

It is the 1880s and Reuben Thompson's horse bus, with driver and solitary passenger on top, stands at Hunters Bar. The road surface was made of limestone. In winter the road was churned up by the horses and wagons into a sea of mud and in summer it became a mass of white dust.

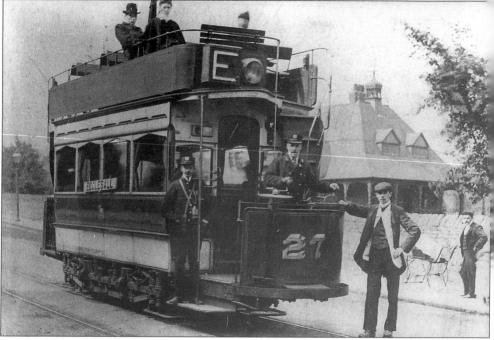

One of the first electric tramcars stands at the Hunters Bar terminus in 1900. Its indicator board says Ecclesall but this point was not reached for some years. The driver and conductor are wearing the original 'pill box' hats. The uniforms were provided by the Corporation, a big improvement on the company days when warm winter clothing was a heavy expense for staff.

A No. 37 at Hunters Bar, probably in 1900 just after the electric trams came on to Ecclesall Road but before the large route letter indicators were provided.

Progress. The year is 1910 and a steam-driven lorry passes a horse and cart in Greystones Road. Note the lorry's iron-clad front wheels.

Two of the new covered trams await passengers at Hunters Bar.

The junction of Psalter Lane and Ecclesall Road at Banner Cross in August 1883. Just up Psalter Lane, in front of the man on a horse is the faint outline of the toll gate across the turnpike from Sheffield. A little further up Ecclesall Road, at the junction with Brincliffe Edge Road, there was a chain, or catch bar, across the road to catch those who had avoided the toll gate by coming up Ecclesall Road.

A little further up the road and twenty-five years later. A tram stands at the Ecclesall terminus at Banner Cross, not long after the route was extended up the hill from Hunters Bar.

A Nether Green tram on its way past Hunters Bar in the early 1900s.

Battey's bus stands outside the Robin Hood hotel at the bottom of Millhouses Lane. The company operated a service to Baslow and Bakewell and in about 1925 Sheffield Corporation became interested in providing a service to Ecclesall.

Pioneer Reg Wyles is pictured at the wheel of a 1907 Darracq French tourer when he was chaffeur to the Kingsford Wilsons at Kingscote House, later renamed Weetwood House. Reg was one of the first people in Sheffield to drive a petrol-engine car. There were only about six in the city at the turn of the century.

Changing times. A pony and trap and a new sports car stand outside the new Wheatsheaf Hotel at Parkhead in the early 1930s.

The first school buses in Sheffield? These new Daimlers replaced the old horse-drawn wagonettes which were used to take children to the open-air school at Whiteley Woods. There was plenty of fresh air for the children who had to sit on top.

The first trams reached Ecclesall terminus in 1922. For years there had been much controversy over extending the tramway from Banner Cross as the wealthy people in the neighbourhood opposed the plan and the upheaval it would cause. Here we see a still very rural Millhouses Lane with Ecclesall Hall Farm on the right and Montgomery house, built in 1914, on the left.

This scene is a far cry from Ecclesall today. Only one car is parked in the street in the late 1920s and it belongs to Alan Ramsay, son of the builder Walter Ramsay, who proudly poses with his wife beside the new automobile before going for a spin.

The Simplex car was manufactured in Sheffield in a factory bought by Earl Fitzwilliam in 1913. He was chairman and sole proprietor until 1924, when the business was bought by Paul Kuehnrich who lived at Holly Court, Ecclesall. Although a new car was produced after the First World War, demand gradually declined. Here Lord Riverdale, who owned one of the very few Simplex cars left in the world, is pictured at the wheel in the 1980s.

Two loves of his life. Gordon Macdonald is pictured in 1934 with his beloved Austin Seven and Grace Partridge, the lady who became his wife, at his then home in Muskoka Drive, Bents Green.

A charabanc belonging to J. and W. Kavanagh of Ecclesall Road is filled with boys and staff, believed to be from Lyndhurst School, ready for an outing in 1923.

A Leyland double-decker is pictured outside the Rising Sun on its introduction in 1957. This bus, YWA 827, was finally withdrawn from service in 1969.

Five

Ecclesall at War

ERECTED BY
SHEFFIELD R.A.F. ASSOCIATION
IN MEMORY OF
THE TEN CREW OF U.S.A.A.F. BOMBER
WHICH CRASHED IN THIS PARK
22·2·1944
PER ARDUA AD ASTRA

Physically, Ecclesall escaped relatively unscathed in both world wars. In the First World War a zeppelin flew overhead as far as Common Lane, turned back and dropped its bombs elsewhere. In the Second World War a few bombs were dropped in the district. However, as in every parish, town and city, memorials pay tribute to those who made the ultimate sacrifice. This one in Endcliffe Park commemorates ten brave airmen.

Fall out! Men of the Sheffield City Battalion break for a rest at Ringinglow during a route march from their base in Edmund Drill Hall in 1915.

The year is 1916 and the newspaper placards outside this newsagents and tobacconist's shop on Ecclesall Road, just below the Greystones Cinema, strike an upbeat note. The *Sheffield Independent* and *Sheffield Telegraph* tell of a German submarine rammed and sunk by a British destroyer and the *Daily Sketch* promises 'The most wonderful war pictures ever taken'.

Members of the Boys Brigade of Wycliffe Church Mission in Hickmott Road pose with a First World War field gun in Bingham Park in 1920. Wilf Mottram, of High Storrs Road, the boy pictured at the top, believes that he is the only member of the group surviving today.

Digging for victory in the First World War. Frederick Richmond was one of the first allotment holders at High Storrs. In the background is a view of Greystones as it was before housing development took place. The allotments were kept up after the war and often turned into gardens. One had a model railway, another a model village and another had a miniature working water wheel.

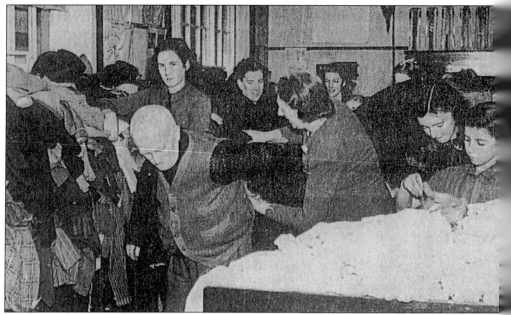

Victims of the Sheffield Blitz are fitted out with new clothes to replace those lost when their homes were bombed. There was no shortage of volunteers to help them at this relief centre set up in High Storrs School. The girl in the right foreground is Joan Hardy who later married the Revd Burnett, vicar of St Mary's.

Classrooms at the school were also turned into a rest centre and here a young soldier helps to entertain some of the young children who found themselves homeless after the bombing.

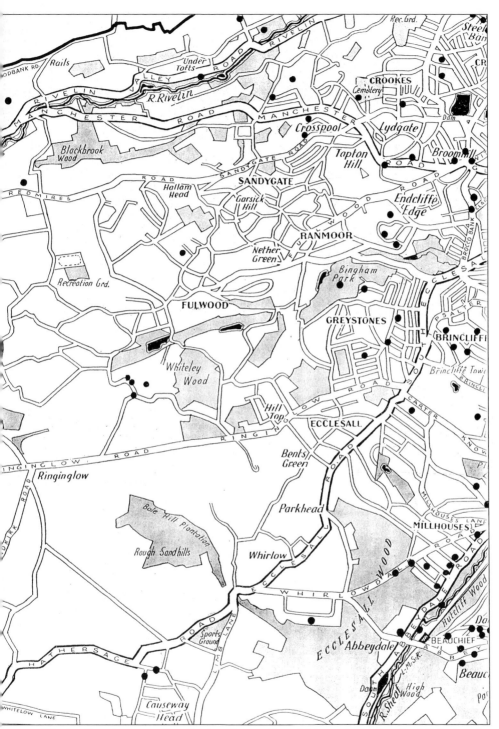

A map of Ecclesall and surrounding districts shows where high-explosive bombs fell during the Second World War. It is taken from the Sheffield Telegraph and Star publication *Sheffield at War* in December 1948.

The horrors of war came to Ecclesall on 22 February 1944. *Mi Amigo*, an American Army A[ir?]
Force B17 crashed in Endcliffe Park as it tried to limp home to its base after being hit during [a?]
bombing mission to Denmark. None of the crew survived. Pictured on an earlier mission the[y?]
were, back row, from left to right: S.Sgt Estabrooks, engineer, Sgt Robbins, tail gunner, S.S[gt]
Mayfield, radio operator, Sgt Ambrosio, engineer, Sgt Tuttle, turret gunner, Sgt Williams, wai[st]
gunner. Front row: Lt Hernandez, bombadier, Lt Humphrey, navigator, Lt Curtis, co-pilot, L[t]
John G. Kriegshauser, pilot. Anthony Thorold, who now lives in Fulwood, met Lt Krieghauser[']
family by chance when he was stationed in the United States with the Fleet Air Arm. Th[e]
family later corresponded with his mother in Sheffield and sent her this photograph.

A memorial was erected in the park to the crew of *Mi Amigo* and anniversary services are held. Here members of ex-servicemen's organisations raise their standards at the fortieth anniversary ceremony in 1984.

Raymond Groves from Fulwood was a thirteen year old schoolboy at the time and one of the first on the scene. He was waiting for a tram at Hunters Bar and saw the Flying Fortress crash into the trees. When he arrived it was burning fiercely. Bullet holes were stitched across the fuselage and there was no sign of life. Ammunition was exploding but he felt no sense of danger until someone told him to get clear. This picture was taken later that year.

A family at war. Typical of the households who did their bit during the Second World War were the Peacocks of Bents Green. Father, George Peacock (centre) was deputy warden of the local ARP, son Fred (left) was in the Home Guard Ack-Ack and his brother John was a member of the ATC. Mother Hylda, a pianoforte teacher, founded the Bents Green Knitting Circle and soon had over 100 volunteers supplying garments for the Forces.

A mother and daughter survey the charred floorboards on the landing of their Ecclesall home after an incendiary device came through the roof.

Pictured is the Thursday platoon of the 65 (West Riding) Home Guard battalion, whose headquarters were in the stables at Mylnhurst School. Nearly all of them signed on in May 1940 at Major Tyzack's Little London Works. Their post on Thursday nights was at the Oxstones on Ringinglow where they kept watch for paratroopers. The sergeant in the centre is Harry Gordon Thorold who was later commissioned second lieutenant and put in charge of the stores. This meant being on duty every evening but at least it was in warmer surroundings than a Thursday night at Oxstones. Among those in the group are: Cpl J. Willoughby (front row, extreme left), W.G. Harrison, E.R. Hodgson, F. Sheldrake, E.G. Credland, C.S. Hiller, S.T. Wright, T. Parker, R.S. Menzie, A.W. King, A. Alexander, J.M.H. Booth.

In September 1941, the men of the Hallamshire sector of the Home Guard worked on a roadblock in the area during a mobilisation exercise. The officer on the left is the sector's commander, Colonel F.A. Neill.

The Civil Defence wardens of Post SK4, which was based at Snaithfield House on Millhouses Lane, are pictured in 1943 with post warden Frank Martin, centre of the front row. The post's area included parts of Ecclesall and their big moment came when a bomb fell on Ecclesall Woods, near the Post Office Sports Ground. It caused little damage however.

Six
Sport and Leisure

This rural scene before the turn of the century looks across Rustlings Road towards Endcliffe Woods and what was to become Endcliffe Park, where generations of city dwellers have come for rest and relaxation. The final five and a half acres of the park were presented to the city by Lt Col H.K. Stephenson, at a ceremony on 12 September 1927.

A hot summer Sunday in Endcliffe Woods and what better way to spend it than going for a row on the boating dam.

In the winter of 1894 the young and not-so-young take advantage of the ice to skate on the pond, enjoying themselves in Endcliffe Park.

'Look Gladys, there's a man with one of those cameras.' Two pretty maids in their Sunday best
are caught by the camera as they take a stroll through Endcliffe Woods around the turn of the
century.

Hot summer days almost a century ago, though in some ways little has changed. Youngsters still
love to paddle in the stream and play with the water as these boys did in the River Porter near
the stepping stones in Endcliffe Park. In the background some young ladies ignore the watery
antics of these lesser mortals.

No shortage of spectators for this tournament at the Hallamshire Tennis Club in 1902. The club, which adjoins Endcliffe Park, was formed in the 1880s.

A Sunday morning stroll through Endcliffe Park in the early part of the century. The bandstand has gone, as well as the fencing alongside the path, but the same café still provides refreshment for the walkers.

Members of the Hill Top chapel, Bents Green, pose before their outing to Sherwood Forest, in 1921. The front row is made up of the Sunday school including, from second left: Alf Hague, Henry Royles, Ernest Royles, Kelly Hague, Stuart Fearn, John Fearn, Arthur Unwin, Joshua Needham, Cecilia Hague, Irene Broomhead, Ethel Chidgey, Bill Chidgey and Ernest Hague. Mrs Lee Naylor, third from left in the third row back, laid one of the foundation stones for the new Bents Green Methodist church which was opened in 1932.

Sunday school children and teachers from the Tin Chapel at Trap Lane, Hill Top, assemble between their banners on Whit Monday in 1917 ready for their parade to Wesley College, now King Edward VII School. In the afternoon they held races and played games in Fearn's field down Trap Lane.

Taking no chances with the weather. These members of St Gabriel's choir are wrapped up for their annual outing to the seaside in 1938. The group includes: Frank Elliot, Hilda Partridge, Tom Croudson, Revd Geoffrey Hick, priest in charge at St Gabriel's, choirmaster Percy Partridge, Paddy Barnett, Doris Fielding, Connie Elliot.

Members of Ecclesall Male Voice Choir rehearse under the baton of their conductor, William Tew, in 1970. The choir was formed in 1951 when Mr Bill Branford of Bents Green advertised in the *Sheffield Telegraph* asking any interested men to report to Banner Cross Methodist church schoolroom. At that time sixteen men joined and over the next twenty years their numbers grew. With Mr Branford as their conductor they won many competitions across the north. Mr Tew took over in 1968 and in 1970 the name was changed to Sheffield Male Voice Choir. In later years numbers dwindled and the choir finally merged with the choir at Dore.

The guiding light of the choir, Bill Branford, with his wife Nellie, on his retirement in 1968. Before forming the choir he was choirmaster at Banner Cross Methodist church for twenty-five years.

Members of St Gabriel's Men's Club dress up for a wedding in one of their concerts in the fifties. Back row, from left to right: Bill Salter, Stan Adams, Gordon Macdonald, Les Todd, Joe Law, Billy Walker. Front row: Mr Darwin, Neil McNab, Norman Sharrat, Horace Knowles, Ken Scott.

St Gabriel's Youth Group in their 1952 production, *Mother Hubbard's Christmas*, which was specially written for the group by Jane Barnett.

One of the May Queen ceremonies at St Gabriel's during the 1950s. The girls are Muriel Wordsworth, Maureen Frith and Mary Roe.

In 1938 the curtain went up on the first production of St Gabriel's Dramatic Society. In the following sixty years the society has had a change of venue, from the church hall to the parish hall on Ringinglow Road, and a change of name – to the Ecclesall Theatre Company. This is a scene from a 1960 production of *She Passed Through Lorraine*.

St Gabriel's wardrobe department excelled itself for this 1963 production of *Pygmalion*.

A dramatic moment from *The Poltergeist*, which the society performed in 1967. In the sixty years since it all began the company has staged more than 160 plays and earned a well deserved reputation for excellence.

The 27th Banner Cross Church Girl Guides was formed in 1933 under the leadership of Miss G. Oram. When she retired in 1945 the company was taken over by Miss Doris Arnold who retired in 1979. She is pictured centre left, with commissioner Mrs Win Longden.

Doris Arnold at her retirement party with Judith Wakefield who was the company's first Queen's Guide. For many years Miss Arnold kept the Silver Hill Dairy.

The 20th Sheffield (Ecclesall church) Scout Group at camp in 1914. The group was formed three years earlier by Mr A.J. Cooper of Whirlow Lane and Mr A. Corker of Parkhead. Research by past honorary group leader Jim Buckley shows that the original group probably met at the old grinding mill at Whirlow Bridge and camped at Whirlow Farm. By 1919 the group had use of the woodwork room at Ecclesall Church School, before moving to the present Scout room in the parish hall.

In 1931 the group celebrated its twentieth anniversary and the Scout room at Ecclesall Church School was specially decorated for the occasion. Rover Scout leader, Charles New, painted murals. In addition the neckerchief was reintroduced in its present form, including the badge of Sir Ralph de Ecclesall's coat of arms.

(Right) Ecclesall Tennis Club's family fun day in 1935. The club was formed in the 1920s and had five grass courts sited between Dunkeld Road and Carterknowle road, near the Prince of Wales.

(Below left) Game and set, but they don't match. Two members of the tennis club pose for a comic shot.

(Below right) Two of the club members dress up for a 'men's day' event.

Spectators line the ground and even sit on the roadside verges to watch this match during Parkhead Cricket Club's festival in 1948. Cricket was played at this ground many years before that and the pitch is shown on photographs dating from around 1904.

Parkhead Cricket Club was founded in 1935 and its 'cricket weeks' began in 1940 as a way of raising money for the war effort. Pictured are the Parkhead and Yorkshire teams who played for one of the festival games in 1948.

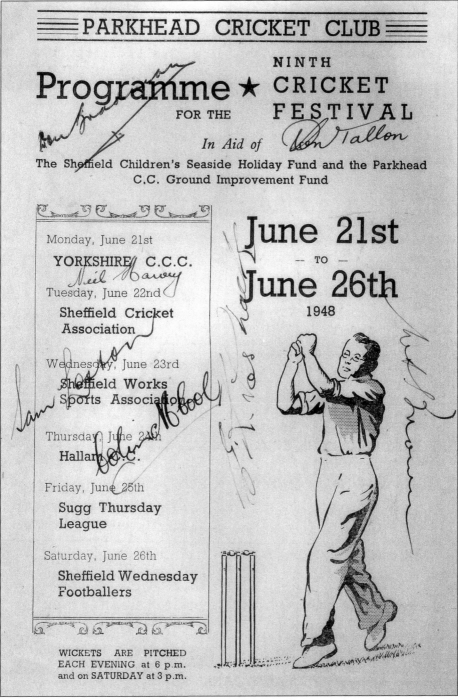

PARKHEAD CRICKET CLUB

Programme ★ NINTH CRICKET
FOR THE FESTIVAL

In Aid of

The Sheffield Children's Seaside Holiday Fund and the Parkhead
C.C. Ground Improvement Fund

Monday, June 21st

YORKSHIRE C.C.C.

Tuesday, June 22nd

Sheffield Cricket Association

Wednesday, June 23rd

Sheffield Works Sports Association

Thursday, June 24th

Hallam C.C.

Friday, June 25th

Sugg Thursday League

Saturday, June 26th

Sheffield Wednesday Footballers

June 21st
— TO —
June 26th
1948

WICKETS ARE PITCHED
EACH EVENING at 6 p.m.
and on SATURDAY at 3 p.m.

Few of the older members of the community will forget the Australian cricketers coming to
England in 1948 – Don Bradman's last visit as a Test player. Yorkshire was playing at Parkhead
and a number of the Aussie players decided to come and watch. Seven of them signed this
programme for a delighted spectator: Don Bradman, Don Tallon, Neil Harvey, Sam Loxton,
Colin McCool, E. Toshak, W.A. Brown.

Ecclesall CSC First Eleven in 1924. The team played on the club ground at Plumpton, an area of land that now forms part of the Silverdale School grounds. Well known local personalities in this photograph include, Fred Naylor (back right) and Lee Naylor (back left). There is also Charles Henry Stokes and John Thomas Stokes. Other families, each with two members pictured are the Hancocks and Corkers.

High Storrs School's first soccer eleven for the 1938/39 season with the captain, Edward Cattell pictured on the front row, centre.

Seven
Royal Visitors

The Prince and Princess of Wales visited St Luke's Nursing Home in March 1984. Here Prince Charles meets the matron, Marjorie Cockburn, while the medical director, Professor Eric Wilkes introduces Princess Diana to other guests.

Princess Diana talks to patients and members of staff, including occupational therapist Ann Holland, while holding a cuddly toy made by one of the patients.

In 1975 the Duchess of Kent formally opened the day unit of St Luke's Hospice. It was eight years earlier that Professor Eric Wilkes gathered together a group of people to raise money to build a special hospital for the relief of the terminally ill. British Steel gave two acres of land on Little Common Lane and in October 1971 St Luke's, the first hospice outside London, opened with its first patients. Here Professor Wilkes introduces Rosalind Beetham, the voluntary help organiser, some of the volunteers, staff and young visitors, to the duchess.

'Who's that with Mr Aiken?' One calf appeared to be asking its minder this when Princess Anne visited Whirlow Hall Farm in July 1980. She was shown around by Alan Aiken, chairman of the Farm Trust which was established in 1979 to provide Sheffield children, particularly the handicapped and disadvantaged, with the chance to learn about farm life and the countryside.

Princess Anne receives a bouquet from seven-year-old Kathryn Marsden.

The Princess stops to watch children working on garden plots. Whirlow Hall was the ancient home of the Bright family. The present Hall, where the children are accommodated when they come to stay for a few days, was built in 1843.

Princess Alexandra opened Silverdale Secondary School in March 1957. Here she chats to two of the pupils, Malcolm Anderson and Leigh Fletcher.

Eight

Epitaphs

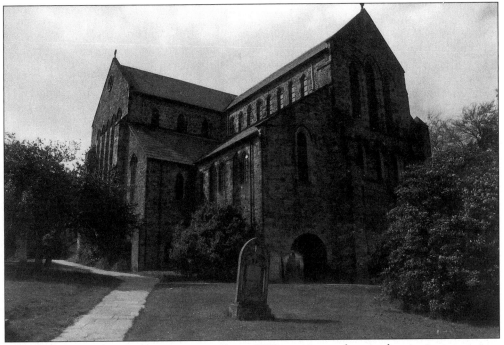

When the new church was consecrated in 1789, a piece of ground covering two acres surrounding it to the south, east and west was also consecrated as a burial ground. This land had been set aside by the Enclosures Act. The first interment is to be found on the south side, that of Benjamin Hill aged five years. In 1969-70 the area was landscaped for ease of maintenance and to improve the setting of the church. Stones were buried or removed to nearby positions.

IN HALLOWED REMEMBRANCE
JOHN MUNRO A.M.L.L.D.
PRINCIPAL OF ECCLESALL COLLEGE
WHO DEPARTED THIS LIFE MARCH 13
1866, IN THE 58TH YEAR OF HIS AGE
AND OF CATHERINE DOWNING
MUNRO, HIS WIFE WHO DIED MAY 8TH
1875 IN THE 58TH YEAR OF HER AGE.
ALSO OF MARY CATHERINE

Dr John Munro (1808-1866) was the principal of the Boys School, Stone Grove, which moved from Westbourne in 1958 and became Ecclesall College. After Dr Munro's death his wife, Catherine Downing Munro, became the proprietress of the school with Samuel Downing Roome as the headmaster. The grave of Samuel Downing Roome of Lincoln (1815-1873) is situated next to theirs. The college closed in 1880.

In
GRATEFUL REMEMBRANCE
of
ELIZ. THE WIFE OF G. BARTIN
of Broad Oak School
DIED JUNE 17, 1825 IN THE
25 YEAR OF HER AGE.
ALSO SARAH, ONLY CHILD OF
THE ABOVE NAMED, WHO
DIED DEC 22, 1830 AGED 9 YEARS

George Bartin (1797-1854) of Broad Oak School lies buried near the west door of the church. The school was founded as a charity school in 1729 and about fourteen children received a basic education from Mr Bartin. George's wife died at the age of twenty-five, their daughter, Sarah, died aged nine and George's son died in 1855, aged eleven. This is a graphic illustration of the early mortality of those days.

The top part of the burial ground contains the graves of many who fought in the two world wars. Among them is Sgt Arnold Loosemore VC DCM of the 8th Duke of Wellington Regiment. He died in 1924, aged twenty-seven. 'Awaiting Reveille'.

Mrs Mary Sarah Hague of Castle Dyke (1853-1938) donated the money to buy land at Greystones for the new church of St Gabriel. The legacies of Miss Enid Gertrude Hague (1882-1942), also buried here, helped to pay for the renewal of the nave at Ecclesall parish church in 1964.

(Above left) William Furness (1817-1895) took over the tenancy of Whirlow Hall when he married Mary Dungworth in 1843. He was the son of Richard Furness of Eyam, the first schoolmaster at Dore, and combined the running of the farm with scythe-making.

(Above right) Henry Vickers (1807-1882) was the son of Benjamin Vickers of Millsands where the great family business, the River Don Works, started. Henry, however, joined the legal profession. He represented Ecclesall Ward on the town council, became mayor and attended Ecclesall church, where the window of the Good Samaritan in the north side of the nave is dedicated to his memory. He had Holmwood built at Parkhead in 1858, a time when many merchants and professional people were moving out to the western suburbs. In the grave at the foot of his family tomb, lies Martha Parkin, 'for more than 40 years faithfully attached to the family of Mr Henry Vickers of Holmwood'.

(Left) Robert Hadfield (1831-1888), who shares the family vault with his cousin, Sir John Brown, founded the firm for the making of steel castings which is still a household name in Sheffield. Meadowhall Shopping Centre has been built on the site of Hadfields East Hecla Works. Robert's son, Sir Robert Abbott Hadfield, lived at Parkhead House.

HERE LIES THE BODY OF
RALPH BLAKELOCK SMITH
OF BENTS GREEN LODGE AND FORMERLY OF THRIFT HOUSE
IN THIS PARISH
WHO WAS BORN ON THE 3RD SEPTEMBER 1823 AND DIED 1 AUGUST 1880
AND OF CHARLOTTE ROBINSON OF HILL TOP HOUSE
WHO WAS BORN ON THE 12TH SEPTEMBER 1827
AND DIED 21ST OCTOBER 1925

Ralph Blakelock Smith (1824-1880) was legal advisor to the Sheffield Water Company and fought to keep it out of public control. His duties were onerous following the Sheffield Flood. His father, Albert, transformed the Sun Inn into the fine residence known as Bents Green Lodge. Ralph moved there from Thrift House on his father's death. His grandfather was curate at Ecclesall church from 1801 to 1817.

Sir John Brown (1816-1896) was one of Sheffield's greatest industrial leaders, twice mayor, twice Master Cutler and the first Sheffield steelmaker to be knighted, an honour bestowed in 1867. He built Endcliffe Hall in 1860 but moved to Bromley in Kent in 1893, where he died. He was brought back to Ecclesall churchyard for burial alongside his wife.

This distinctive gravestone can be seen by the path from the lychgate. It marks the grave of an unknown artist.

Revd George Sandford (1816-1898) spent fifty-five years of his ministry in Sheffield. During his incumbency as vicar of Ecclesall, from 1880 until his death, he obtained an addition of two acres to the churchyard. His grateful parishioners erected the oak lychgate at the entrance to the churchyard in 1903 as a tribute to his memory. His simple grave presents a contrast to the surrounding Victorian family vaults.

John Newton Mappin (1800-1883), 'a benefactor to Sheffield, his native town', was a member of the family of silver engravers and founded a brewery business. He built St John's, Ranmoor and on his death left £15,000 and his art collection to the city. The structure of the Mappin Art Gallery, which opened in 1887, bears a striking resemblance to its benefactor's tomb.

John Brightmore Mitchell Withers (1838-1894) was the architect who designed St Silas', St Andrew's Sharrow, St John's Owlerton, the almshouses at Dore and several schools. He supervised the re-roofing of the State Apartments at Chatsworth and was the architect of several handsome residences, including Broomcroft and Woodlands (later Parkhead House), which he designed for himself.

Acknowledgements

Our grateful thanks are extended to all the kind people who lent photographs and supplie information to make this book possible. They include: Mr M. Arksey, Doris Arnold, Mr D Askham, Grant Barnsley, William Blake, Mrs David Booker, Henry Boot and Sons plc, Jir Buckley, Peter Charlton (editor, *The Star*), the library staff of Sheffield Newspapers, the lat Horace Clayton, John Clifford, Marjorie Delgarno, Stephen Doncaster, Hilary Etchells, Ro Fielding, David Flather, William Franklyn, Shirley Frost, Alvey Graham, Margaret Hadwir Graham Hague, Charles Hall, Peter Harvey, Mollie Hessey, Mary Hickes, Mr and Mrs W Jamieson and the Ecclesall Theatre Company, Alan Jones, Carol Jones, Tim Keating, Gordor MacDonald, Betty McPherson, Donald Martin, Mrs Tom Medley, Wilf Mottram, Mylnhurs School, Brett Naylor, Joshua Needham, Neill Tools Ltd, Parkhead Cricket Club, Fred Peacock Paul Proctor, Mr and Mrs Gordon Ramsay, Mr W. Roberts, Mr and Mrs H. Royles, St Luke Hospice, Margaret Sargeant, Gerald Spink, Audrey Whippey, Molly Wyles and the librarians c the local studies library, for their assistance and for permission to reproduce photographs and sale plan from their collection. If we have inadvertently missed anyone we apologise. Ever effort has been made to discover the copyright of photographs but in some cases this has prove impossible.